FOOD AROUND THE WORLD

Food in India

Polly Goodman

PowerKiDS
press.
New York

Published in 2008 by The Rosen Publishing Group, Inc.
29 East 21st Street, New York, NY 10010

First Edition

Editor: Sarah Gay
Senior Design Manager: Rosamund Saunders
Designer: Tim Mayer
Consultant: Susannah Blake

Library of Congress Cataloging-in-Publication Data

Goodman, Polly.
   Food in India / Polly Goodman. — 1st ed.
       p. cm. — (Food around the world)
   Includes index.
   ISBN 978-1-4042-4296-8 (library binding)
   1. Cookery, Indic—Juvenile literature. 2. Food habits—
India—Juvenile literature. I. Title.
   TX724.5.I4G563 2008
   641.5954—dc22
                                          2007032604

Manufactured in China

Cover photograph: an Indian man selling spices on
the street.

Photo credits: Richard I'Anson/Lonely Planet 6, 10, 22
and 23, Lindsay Brown/Lonely Planet 8, Chris
Beall/Lonely Planet 9, Greg Elms/Lonely Planet 11 and
21, Paul Beinssen/Lonely Planet 12, Lee Studios/Anthony
Blake Photo Library 13 and 26, Dallas Stribley/Lonely
Planet 14, Fabfoodpix 15, Wayland Picture Library 16
and title page, Catherine Karnow/CORBIS 17, Stuart
Freedman/Panos Pictures 18, foodfolio/Alamy 19,
Eaglemoss Consumer Publications/Anthony Blake Photo
Library 20, Dinodia Photo Library 24, DANISH
ISMAIL/Reuters/Corbis 25, Frans Lemmens/zefa/Corbis
cover.

Contents

Words in **bold** can be found in the glossary on page 28

Welcome to India

India is a huge country in Asia. It is famous for its hot, spicy food. Religion is very important in India. It affects what people eat. Most people in India are Hindus, but there are many other religions, including Muslims, Sikhs, Christians, and Buddhists.

▼ *The busy Ganges river in Northern India is very important to Hindus.*

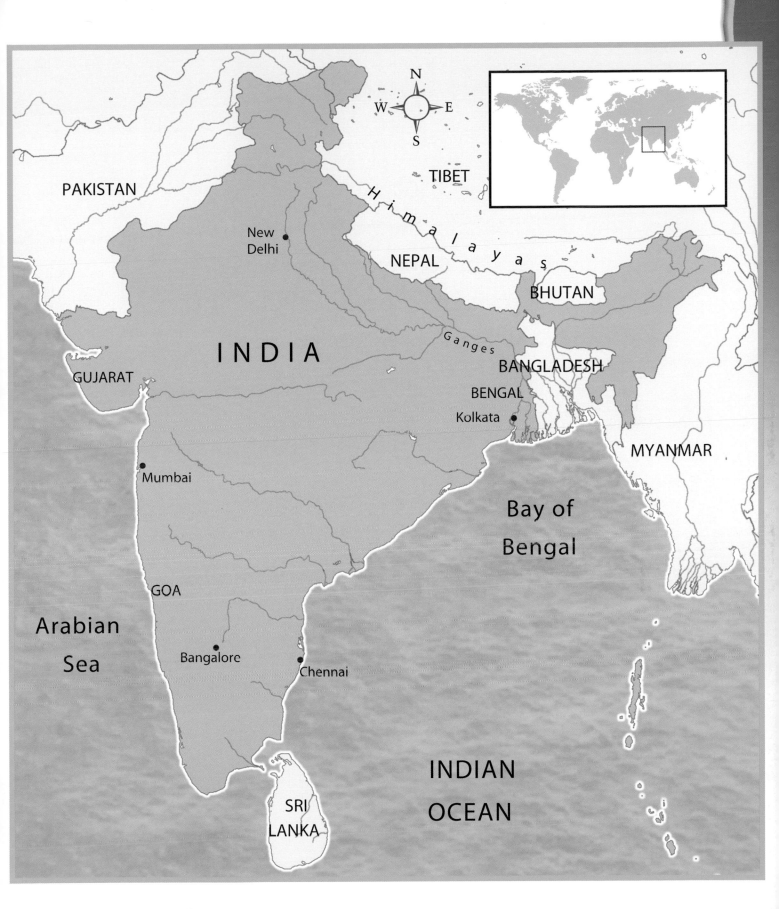

▲ *India is marked on this map in orange.*
Over one billion people live there.

Farming and weather

India stretches over 3,500 mi. (5,600 km), from the Himalayas in the north to the Indian Ocean in the south. Some foods grow well in the cool mountains of Northern India. Other foods grow well in the hot, tropical south.

▼ *Tea grows well in the hot, wet weather of Southern India.*

In Northern India, wheat grows well on the **fertile** plains around the Ganges and Indus rivers. Farther south, rice, spices, and many tropical fruits are suited to the hotter, wetter weather.

▲ **Winnowing** *wheat in Northern India.*

Food fact

Spices come from different plants, such as the capsicum bush, ginger plant, and clove tree.

Bread, rice, and spices

Wheat is ground and made into many different breads. **Pappadams** and **pooris** are fried. **Naans** are cooked in an oven. **Parathas** are flatbreads that are stuffed with potatoes and other fillings. People in India use bread to scoop up their food.

▼ *All kinds of bread are for sale outside this bakery in Northern India.*

▲ This dish, called vegetable pilau, is made from rice, spices, and vegetables.

Rice is cooked in different ways. Pilau is a rice dish flavored with spices and stock. Rice fried with meat, fish, or vegetables is called a biryani. Ground rice is made into rice cakes, called **idlis**.

Vegetables, pulses, and fruit

There are hundreds of vegetable dishes in India. Many include lentils, chickpeas, kidney beans, or other **pulses**. Lentils are cooked with spices to make a sauce called daal. Other vegetables are fried in chickpea batter to make **samosas** or **bhajis**.

◀ *Bhajis, samosas, and spicy chips are for sale at a market stall.*

Tropical fruits, such as mangoes and **papaw**, are made into chutneys. They are served as side dishes. Cucumber and other vegetables are mixed with yogurt to make a dish called a **raita**.

▲ *This raita contains yogurt, cucumber, pepper, mint, and onion.*

Food fact

It's nice and cooling to eat a raita after a hot, spicy dish.

Fish and meat

In coastal towns and villages in India, **pomfret**, mackerel, and other fresh fish are caught and eaten. Bummalo fish are small fish that are dried and made into a dish called **Bombay Duck**. Prawns, mussels, and lobsters are also popular.

◀ Women in Mumbai divide the catch of the day into different types of fish.

Lamb and chicken are the most popular
meats in India. Lamb is often cubed,
marinated, and cooked on a skewer, called
a kebab. Tandoori chicken is marinated in
yogurt and spices, then cooked in a clay
oven, called a tandoor.

▲ Rogan Josh is
a curry usually
made with
lamb, tomatoes,
and spices.

Shopping and street food

Food in India is mostly bought fresh from local markets. Most villages have a bakery, fish shop, butcher, and a general store that sells rice, drinks, and canned foods. Some of the larger towns also have supermarkets.

▼ Chutneys and spices for sale at a market stall.

Street vendors cook and sell pooris,
samosas, **bhelpuris**, and other snacks from
roadside stalls. Some serve fresh, tropical
fruit juices, and a traditional Indian yogurt
drink called **lassi**.

▲ *Lassi is made from yogurt, water, salt, and spices.*

Mealtimes in India

Everyday Indian meals might include dishes from the menus below.

Breakfast

Paratha (pancake stuffed with cheese or vegetables)

Idlis (rice cakes) and a bowl of sambar (spicy soup)

Water

Tea

▼ These men are delivering hot lunch boxes to office workers in the city.

Lunch

Thali (metal tray) containing the following:

Dhal

Okra bhaji (spicy okra)

Matar panir (cheese and peas in a spicy sauce)

Raita potatoes (potatoes and yogurt)

Pickles & chutneys

Rice

Chapatis (flatbreads)

———

Water

Banana lassi

Dinner

Rice

Spicy pulses

Potatoes

Chapatis (flatbreads)

Dosas (pancakes)

———

Fresh fruit

▶ *A thali meal.*

Around the country

There are different cooking styles all over India. In Northern India and in Muslim areas, people eat mainly meat, vegetables, and breads. Spicy lamb dishes such as Rogan Josh are common.

▼ *Tandoori Chicken comes from Northern India.*

In the south, fish is eaten on the coast and rice is part of every meal. Southern dishes often contain tropical fruits and nuts, such as coconut, mangoes, and cashews. In areas with strict Hindus, such as Gujarat, most people are **vegetarian**.

▲ *Dosas are pancakes made from rice and lentil flour. They come from Southern India.*

Special occasions

Indians celebrate important events with special meals. At a Hindu wedding, the guests enjoy a huge feast with over 20 different dishes, including desserts such as kheer (rice pudding) and kulfi (ice cream).

▼ At a Hindu wedding, rice and rose petals are thrown to wish the bride and groom good luck.

When Sikhs go to the temple, they share a meal together in the langer (kitchen). Everyone helps to prepare and serve the food. At a Sikh wedding, a special sweet called **karah prashad** is blessed and passed around before everyone shares a meal.

▲ *In this Sikh temple, everyone helps peel potatoes for a shared meal.*

Festival food

The biggest festival in India is Diwali. It is celebrated by both Hindus and Sikhs. People take gifts of sweets to friends and relatives. They might take jalebis (fried sweets), gulab jamuns (fried milk balls), or barfi (milk fudge).

▼ These plates of barfi and other sweets are ready for Diwali.

◀ Muslims pray together before breaking their fast during Ramadan.

During the month of Ramadan, Muslims **fast** during the hours of daylight. Id-ul-Fitr celebrates the end of Ramadan, and families eat a big lunch together. They eat sweet foods, such as dates, almonds, and cakes.

Food fact

After sunset, Muslims break their Ramadan fast by eating a special meal called Ifthar.

Make a mixed raita!

What you need

1 ½ cups (300g) plain yogurt

1 tablespoon fresh mint leaves

1 small cucumber

1 red pepper

½ onion

¼ teaspoon ground nutmeg

What to do

1. Put the yogurt into a bowl.

2. Chop the mint, cucumber, pepper, and onion and add them to the yogurt.

3. Mix everything together with the nutmeg and serve.

4. Decorate with mint leaves.

Ask an adult to help you make this dish. Always be careful with sharp knives.

A balanced diet

This food pyramid shows which foods you should eat to have a healthy, **balanced diet**.

We shouldn't eat too many fats, oils, cakes, and candies.

Milk, cheese, meat, fish, beans, and eggs help to keep us strong.

We should eat plenty of vegetables and fruit to keep healthy.

Bread, cereal, rice, and pasta should make up most of our diet.

Indian meals use all foods from the pyramid. Some Indian dishes are fried in oil, but most Indian meals are balanced because they contain rice or bread with vegetables, meat, or fish.

Glossary

balanced diet a diet that includes a mixture of different foods, which supplies all the things a body needs to keep healthy

bhaji deep-fried vegetables in batter

bhelpuri a snack made from lentil-flour noodles, puffed rice, and wheat crackers with diced, boiled potatoes and chutneys

Bombay Duck a dish made from dried bummalo fish

digestion the process of breaking down food in the body

fast to go without food

fertile land that is good for growing crops

idlis rice cakes

karah prashad a sweet-tasting pudding made from semolina, sugar, and butter, which has been blessed

lassi a drink made from yogurt

marinated soaked in a sauce to add flavor

naan a thick, baked flatbread

papaw a fruit with orange flesh and small black seeds

pappadam an Indian flatbread made from lentil flour

paratha flatbreads that is often stuffed with a variety of fillings

poori crispy, puffed-up, deep-fried bread

pomfret a saltwater fish

pulses beans, peas, and other foods that are edible seeds

raita a side dish made from yogurt, onion, and mint

samosa deep-fried pastry containing spiced vegetables or meat

vegetarian a person who does not eat meat or fish

winnowing blowing air through wheat to separate the parts you can eat from the parts you can't

Further information

Books to read

A World of Recipes: India by Julie McCulloch (Heinemann, 2001)

Ceremonies and Celebrations: Feasts and Fasting by Kerena Marchant (Raintree, 2001)

Kids Around the World Celebrate!: The Best Feasts and Festivals from Many Lands by Lynda Jones (Jossey-Bass, 1999)

Let's Eat! What Children Eat Around the World by Beatrice Hollyer (Henry Holt and Co, 2004)

Letters From Around the World: India by David Cumming (Cherrytree Books, 2004)

Picture a Country: India by Henry Pluckrose (Franklin Watts, 1998)

Index

All the numbers in **bold** refer to photographs.